LAURENCE FREEMAN OSB (ED.)

Meditation with Children

Revised by Liam Kelly

CONVIVIUMPRESS

MEDITATIO

2013

Meditation with Children

© World Community for Christian Meditation
© Laurence Freeman OSB

© Convivium Press 2013

http://www.conviviumpress.com
sales@conviviumpress.com
convivium@conviviumpress.com

7661 NW 68th St, Suite 108,
Miami, Florida 33166. USA.
Phone: +1 (305) 8890489
Fax: +1 (305) 8875463

Edited by Rafael Luciani
Revised by Liam Kelly
Designed by Eduardo Chumaceiro d'E
Series: *Meditatio*

ISBN: 978-1-934996-53-9

Printed in Colombia
Impreso en Colombia
D'VINNI, S.A.

Convivium Press
Miami, 2013

Meditation with Children

Contents

Chapter 1

Does God have Favourites?

LAURENCE FREEMAN OSB

Welcome to our first Meditatio seminar in this new outreach of our community as we approach the twentieth anniversary of the founding of the World Community in its present form.

I once asked this question —does God have favourites— of a wise old Rabbi. He thought about it for a few moments, and he said that as a young man he believed definitely God had favourites. God's favourites were the chosen race, the chosen people, the Jews. In middle age he reconsidered this and he came to realise that God had no favourites, that God's love was equally distributed to all. Jesus tells us «Your heavenly father causes the sun to rise on good and bad alike and sends the rain on the innocent and the wicked». So no favouritism there. But then this old Rabbi said to me, «In old age I've come back to my original perception to believe that God does have favourites, but now I sense that the favourites of God are the *anawim*, the poor ones of the earth, the ones who are voiceless, the ones who are neglected, the ones who are oppressed».

Jesus did give a special attention or point out a special significance to two groups: the *anawim*, the poor, the neglected, the oppressed, the marginalised, and children. On one occasion, he pointed to a child to illustrate the very heart and essence of his teaching, his message, which was about the simplicity and the powerlessness of the Kingdom of God.

This is from the Gospel of Luke:

> *An argument started among them as to which of them*
> *was the greatest. Jesus who knew what was going on in*
> *their minds took a child stood him by his side and said*
> *«Whoever receives this child in my name receives me*
> *whoever receives me receives the one who sent me because*
> *the least among you all is the greatest* (Luke 9:46-48).

I think this moment in the Gospel story is a very telling one in our seminar today and for the work our Community has begun in teaching meditation to children in schools particularly. There are 21 countries in our Community where there is an active programme for teaching Christian meditation in schools. Here's another quotation of Jesus we could use to describe his own understanding of a child and the importance of a child:

Unless you become like a little child you will never enter the Kingdom of Heaven (Matt 18:3).

This is one we might use when we are speaking about meditation and try to explain in as few words as possible the simplicity of meditation. John Main's great emphasis on the simplicity of the practice, the goal, and the means consistent with the goal, are all simple. Meditation is challenging; it is not easy because it is simple. I think this one about taking the child and saying whoever receives this child in my name receives me is particularly useful because it points out the essential difference between the child-like and the grown-up state, the difference between the child and the adult. And it also speaks of the need to «receive» the child which we might say today how to relate to them, how to respond to them, how to be responsible to them and for them. To receive children.

How do we receive children in our society? In our culture we are intensely sensitive about that today for all sorts of reasons. We are conscious of how easily we can destroy childhood, abuse it in the many forms of abuse that leave lifelong wounds in the psyche. So how do we receive a child? How do we relate to them? These sayings of Jesus give us an important insight into the meaning of education today and the reason why we should as a matter of urgency teach meditation to children today.

Think about these words of Jesus as we prepare to learn more about the spirituality of education and the spiritual life of children. This is our adult responsibility to teach and form children. I think most parents I've met suffer from a sense of failure, a sense of constantly feeling they could have done better, or should have done something they forgot to do or weren't able to do and I'm sure teachers feel this a lot of the time as well, such an overwhelming responsibility and such a delightful one when we feel that we are at least beginning to fulfil it. So it is our responsibility to teach and inform children but in doing so we learn, we have to learn from them. No teacher could teach effectively unless she or he is learning from the people they are teaching. This is why the Holy Spirit is active in any teaching relationship as a mutuality, a reciprocity. And if there isn't that two-way transfer of that wisdom, knowledge, experience, then teaching is just instruction or indoctrination or sort of mechanical training, technical training. Teaching involves a relationship. It is a relationship in which the optimum distance has to be respected —that there are different roles in the relationship which have to be maintained— but there is a mutual benefit.

I think in teaching children we can learn what we need to know in order to recover our own spiritual balance today. There is a very widespread sense that there is something wrong, something unbalanced, not only with our economy but with many institutions of our society and even of the foundations of our understanding of what society is and how it should operate. There's something gone out of sync; there's something unbalanced.

Teaching meditation to children may be a much more powerful way of re-balancing the whole system that we operate in than we may think at first. In the mystical tradition St. Gregory of Nyssa for example, tells us every image of God, every idea of God, is an idol, is a barrier, a false god. I think it is part of our contemporary spirituality that we seek a God beyond this kind of dualism, beyond this kind of judgementalism. We seek God who speaks to us beyond words in the direct intimacy of silence, and free from the mental constructs of our own imagination, our own desires and fears, so that this God we are seeking is not a projection of our own ego, our own woundedness. A God who can be truly experienced both in transcendence and in imminence. God within and beyond us. And in that discovery to find our own healing and wholeness and holiness. So a God of mystery, God of immediacy, God of present-ness. It is this capacity of a child to be immediate, to be naturally and totally present in the moment, that makes us sense that in some way children are closer to God than we are, or that there is less of an opaque barrier between the child and God than there is with most of us. This capacity of a child to be present is the capacity of the child for pure prayer, for contemplation, for meditation, for the prayer of the heart.

Chapter 2

The Capacity for Contemplation

LAURENCE FREEMAN OSB

Meditation is simple and natural and good for us. Medical science the past sixty years assures us of this. Every week there is a new research document out speaking about the benefits of meditation. So does the spiritual wisdom of all traditions for several millennia. We learn today that children respond to meditation very naturally, enthusiastically, and they like it. They can meditate and they like to meditate. Perhaps many of us got interested in meditation later in life, as a way of deepening our prayer, looking for a more contemplative dimension; once you get the taste of God you want more of it, you want to go deeper. Or perhaps, a psychiatrist or a GP told you when you went to see them about your cholesterol or your stress levels, why not try meditation? For whatever reason we might meditate we find it challenging, we find it difficult.

As soon as we start to get into it as a serious discipline we begin to touch some kind of limit within ourselves. That is what every discipline brings us to; every discipline brings us to a stage of transcendence, going beyond ourselves. Discipline is not easy for us because it challenges us. It is meant to challenge us. We would not grow unless we were challenged, unless we were pushing back those limitations. It challenges the very root of our ego. This is the fundamental spiritual understanding of meditation, that it takes us beyond our ego. And the difference between the child and the adult is simply the density and the complexity, the historical form of the ego. Children have egos but we put up with them; we might even find them amusing provided you don't have to live with them. At different ages the ego of the child takes different forms of expression. As adults we argue intensely about who is the greatest as the disciples of Jesus were doing in the Gospel story and we jostle for superiority.

As we come into the world, we come into a jungle of competition. We teach competitiveness to children at a very young age, younger and younger. And children, too, of course, can be jealous and competitive and feel superior to each other, but their ego is generally much less dense, more easily transcended, and they can pass much more smoothly and quickly from competition to collaboration. This was one thing that Jesus was trying to say in that teaching moment when he confronted the political egos of his disciples —who was going to get the best cabinet places in the Kingdom. The other thing he is saying I think is that we have to learn how to «receive a child in my name». That's a subtle phrase, it's not a magic formula. «In my name» refers to a relationship. To receive a child in my name is to receive the God within them, you might say. And in receiving the God within them we are also becoming more aware of the God within ourselves. So receiving a child «in his name» is to receive him and also the God whom he carries within himself.

This makes us think, as we should do in this difficult transition of Christianity as an institution, the system of belief as a social force makes us think about the meaning of prayer. Any teacher or parent knows the extraordinary direct holiness and goodness in a child, and to accept and to receive that is immediately to be put into touch with a higher power, a higher or purer level of consciousness. Higher, simpler, purer, more transparent, more disarming, than our egos are used to. The fragility and the vulnerability of a child is also strangely enough then the medium for an amazing power and strength —one of the great paradoxes of the human person.

It is indeed an experience of God. To teach, to raise children is a spiritual experience however we may understand it. Whatever kind of system we may be using, however we may professionalise it, the teaching or the raising of a child is a spiritual experience. It's a value of universal currency, it transcends all cultures and it's why teaching and parenthood are vocations of the highest order. To receive a child in this way reminds us of our own true selves.

I was visiting school in the Townsville diocese a couple of years ago. We were making a film; I was wearing my white monastic habit. As the children were running around getting their meditation space ready as they did everyday setting up the little circle and putting the prayer bear in the middle of the circle and lighting the candle and doing this with real enthusiasm and joy, I noticed there was one little girl maybe six or seven years old who was not engaged in all this frenetic activity but was just looking at me in my white habit, with this look of utter and total amazement. So I looked at her and said «Hello, what's your name?» She just didn't hear me at all; she just continued to stare. She was just staring at me. And then she said «Are you an angel?»

A few minutes later we were sitting next to each other in the circle, meditating for five minutes, one minute per year of their age. And I thought afterwards, we were both doing the same thing. She was meditating in exactly the same way that I was. I'm sure she was meditating much better than I was and I'm sure she was much closer to God than I was. Each of us at our own place in the journey of human development, she in this mythical magical world still, me in wherever I was at. In the same space we could occupy doing the same work of being in the present moment, of moving from mind to heart, each in our own way to our own capacity. That moment condensed, concentrated, for me a great deal of what I think we're going to be listening to today.

We see present before us in the child the capacity for the direct experience of truth. Our later ego development often blocks and confuses this perception. That is why it's so important for us to receive a child, to relate to a child, like Jesus not like ourselves. We should not project our own complexities on to a child because this is the beginning of an abuse of their childlikeness. We are treating them as adults if we do that, which they are not.

We should see in them the simple capacity for contemplation. We should see their simple capacity for
contemplation as a gift. We see that this gift is something *we* still possess with all our ego complexities,
with all our complex questionings, with all our failure or self-rejection. We should see in their simple
capacity for contemplation the gift that we may
have lost touch with but is still recoverable.

Chapter 3

The Benefits and the Spiritual Fruits of Meditation

LAURENCE FREEMAN OSB

Children are capable of pure prayer. The early Christians called it pure prayer —the real meaning of meditation. Therefore, we should not limit them in our spiritual or religious education just to techniques of relaxation, or imaginative prayer, or guided meditations. We should not limit them to that just as we should not limit them to just moral instruction or catechism or doctrinal information. All those are good and useful, necessary things, but they are not the whole picture. They are not the most direct and intuitive thing that the child is capable of in their relationship with God. The child can go much deeper than this. And if we teach them to do so, even with the limited experience of it ourselves, they will surely teach us in return about the capacity that we have that we have dangerously forgotten.

This is why the spiritual roots of meditation in religious traditions are important, and it is why there is a difference between different kinds of meditative practices within those traditions. We shouldn't confuse those different levels of prayer. Just because we may have got alienated or cut off from this capacity for contemplation, it should not lead us to believe that the child couldn't do it either. That would be to sell them very short and to miss the grace of this encounter with children that is part of the human generational process. There may be situations in which a purely secular approach to meditation is the best. and you can leave God out of it entirely, you don't have to link it to any religious tradition or spiritual language. There may be situations where you can do that, that's the best.

We can approach meditation just as a technique for gaining physical and psychological benefits. Medical research in this field is conclusive. Meditation is good for you, the scientists tell us. But meditation was not invented by these researchers. Herbert Benson, founder of the Mind/Body Medical Institute at Massachusetts General Hospital, wrote *The Relaxation Response* in 1975. That is the same year that we started the meditation centre in London. He wrote the book to prove, from his research, the benefits of meditation as a purely secular psychological technique, physical technique, in reducing stress. In 1984 he wrote a follow-up called *Beyond the Relaxation Response*. In this later research he showed that the benefits that he had itemised in the previous work were enhanced by practising meditation in the religious or spiritual context. He did this without any bias himself, purely objective research. You got more of the benefits if you believed in something or you meditated within some religious framework.

Meditation naturally belongs to this common spiritual wisdom of humanity and its fullest meaning is to be discovered there. The benefits are indisputable, but as well as the benefits you have the spiritual fruits of meditation and these are described and attested by the mystical research of many millennia. Whereas cholesterol under control, blood pressure, insomnia, anxiety, immune systems, stress, depression, panic attacks, memory, self-esteem, cancer treatment, are all beneficially affected by meditation, the spiritual fruits love, joy, peace, patience, kindness, goodness, gentleness, fidelity, and self-control, and an awareness of our essential goodness, are results that move the very horizons of our being, of our perception, because they lead us to a self-knowledge that transcends the ego and leads to the threshold of the knowledge of God.

Competitiveness and consumerism are egotistical, egotistically-centred activities. Me, my desire, my fear, my image these are egotistic co-activities intensely developed in our culture. We are really trained for these things —only winners make it. And we teach this to children at a very, very young age, to be consumers, to be competitive, to win. It is vital that in this culture climate we are actively intervening to give children an awareness based upon experience, because with young children you don't conceptualise this but you give them an experiential opportunity of being aware that there is another way of relating to themselves and others. Somebody sent me a note from one of the countries where meditation is being taught. They said «On October 28th the Annual Spelling Bee was held at Santa Elena School (in South America). Once more the children opened the event with a short meditation. Not only did the school authorities attend but also the zone supervisor, an important representative from the Ministry of Education, as well as the Channel 9 TV station. Competition got quite difficult. One of the children at one point said to the coordinator «Now is the time we should meditate».

Meditating in a spiritual tradition offers us a support system, a community, and a context of spiritual friendship which are vital to the experience of being human and of human growth because these fruits of meditation help us to persevere in the discipline of the practice. This is what learning to meditate in a school environment teaches us, and the children as well. Go back to your own memories of your classmates in school. I went through many years of school from the age of seven, moving with more or less the same group of friends, and we became very close in a way. Not as close to everybody as to some obviously, but it was a sense of a very strong identity with our group. That is one of the first experiences that children have of bonding in a social environment outside of their own family. If they can learn and they do learn to meditate with that group and in that group, as part of that group, in the classroom, they are learning something of immense benefit for their social relationships later in life. They can recognise that the labels and the caricatures and the ways we marginalise or characterise individuals in our group are not absolute labels, these are not absolute forms of relationship, that we can go beyond those. Sitting in meditation for 5, 10, 15 minutes with that regular group has an immense impact upon the formation of our sense of belonging to society.

Meditation in a school setting can be adapted of course to a single faith. It can also be practised in a purely secular way or in a class of mixed faiths. One of the advantages of the way of meditation that we teach, the mantra, is that it is something you find in all religious traditions. Today also we find the post-modern phenomenon of people who don't know what they are in terms of faith identity, or people who have had absolutely no religious formation at all apart from what they have seen on Christmas television. Meditation highlights the distinction between faith and belief and this distinction is of immense importance if we are to answer that question about whether God has favourites or not.

Faith is our capacity for relationship, for commitment, for forgiveness, for transcendence. We need beliefs, we need belief systems, we need rules and regulations, we need boundaries, we need sacred symbols, and these two aspects of our spiritual journey, of faith and belief, are linked and should be happily and in a stimulating way related. But they are distinct. Meditation can be practised in any group because it is purely a way of faith that allows us to live with the diversity of belief.

St. Thomas Aquinas said that the goal and the reward of life is union with God, and he gave a number of definitions of what that meant —union with God. One I like is his 4th characteristic of union with God which he says is «the community of supreme delight in which all share in the same good and all love each other as himself or herself and each rejoices in each other's well-being». That surely must be the goal of education as well, and it explains the importance of teaching meditation to children, because meditation brings us into this experience of union with God. It also explains why God has no favourites, because when we become fully alive, fully human, we help each other to flourish. We see that our flourishing, our happiness does not have to be achieved at the expense of others, there's enough to go around because there is in fact an infinite source of this which we call God. So we help each other to flourish and we take delight in each other's being however similar or different we may be. It is the end of competition and the beginning of communion.

Chapter 4

Christian Meditation in Townsville Schools

DR. CATHY DAY

Why we chose to go down the path of being quite daring to introduce Christian Meditation in every one of our schools —a total of 12,000 students— is that we wanted them to have that experience. As far as we know we're the only systemic schooling organisation that has actually done this sort of project, to introduce Christian Meditation in all our schools. I have one benchmark if you like for making decisions and it is very simple: Is it good for all of our students? I felt that with Christian Meditation it was a compelling answer: yes, yes, yes.

We had become meditators, but it's one thing for a couple of us to be enthusiastic about something. It is another thing entirely to go out to your 8 or 900 teachers and say to them, «Hey, we've got something else for you to do today» and expect that they are going to take on board and sort of rush off with it. I think deep down though I had absolute faith that, provided we did this in a way that we had support for teachers, we had formation programmes, that we did the pilot programme, and we allowed those teachers and most students basically to do the talking for us, that it was going to work. Certainly, six years later I can actually attest that it has become something that I think our Catholic schools and the diocese of Townsville are known for. It is a real hallmark of our schools.

I had great faith in our teachers. We have a saying that we have used for a number of years with our staff. We say to our teachers: «Doesn't matter what the government say to us. You our teachers are not mere technicians for that curriculum that is delivered to us to be delivered to students. You are the guardians at the gateway of wonder». That has really resonated with our teachers because they instinctively understand that, within their vocation, that opening the mind and the heart of the child is indeed opening the gateways of wonder. So I thought Christian Meditation was just a very simple way to enhance that vision of what the teacher is in our schools.

However, it wasn't just our teachers that needed to be convinced. I have an education council and basically they advise the bishop, and really the bishop has ultimate authority to give the green light to any of the initiatives that are beyond what the government is mandating in our schools. So I thought I'm going to do a presentation to them to talk about our idea to go beyond the pilot programme and to take that leap of faith, to be daring, and to introduce it to all 12,000 students.

I thought about what I needed to say. The Delors report presented by UNESCO in 1996 has the four pillars of education in their report «Learning the Treasure Within». Even the title screamed to me that it's about the interior education of the heart. So the four pillars: learning to know, learning to do, learning to live together and with others, and learning to *be*. I don't think that's actually in our new Australian curriculum; I wish it was. But I think that in a religious school setting that's where we have the absolute and ultimate authority to draw the line in the sand and to say: We are not just technicians of a curriculum; we want to give our students something that is about educating the heart.

In a Catholic school setting I believe the ultimate way we do that is certainly through our prayer experience, to go beyond the notion that prayer is something to be learned. Prayer is something to be experienced and I think that Christian Meditation prayer of the heart has been a very powerful way for our students to find that still place within where their hearts can expand if you like. That was one point that I certainly put to the council. In fact the UNESCO report went on to say that it is education's noble task to encourage each and every one, acting in accordance with their traditions and convictions and paying full respect to pluralism, to lift their minds, hearts and spirits to the plan of the universal and in some measure to transcend themselves.

Meditation, it is no exaggeration to say that the survival of humanity depends thereon. Very powerful words but I wonder how many people have power in terms of dictating what is going on in schooling, certainly in Australia where we're experiencing much of what has happened in the UK. Governments tend to mandate so much these days, it's becoming very burdensome and I don't know that it is achieving what we would think educating the whole child is about. So if we can just take the time to put some really precious energy into the prayer experiences for our students, I think we're doing them not just a great favour but we're doing the work that God really wants us to do. John Main attests:

Meditation is the way of growth, the way of deepening our own commitment to life, our own maturity. It is the most important priority for every one of us to allow our spirit two things. First, the deepest possible contact with the life source, and then, as a result of that contact, to allow our spirit space within which to expand.

To me it really explains deeply what the experience of prayer is about. What does it mean for us when we say that a high priority in every life that would be truly human should be this contact with this life source? Jesus said: «I have come that you may have life and have it in abundance». What does that mean? What does that mean in terms of what a teacher might do in a classroom with their students to explain that it's better to *be* than to have? To me it's in stark contrast to educating the child to become another producer or consumer for the economy. It is about recognising that the spiritual growth of the child has to be given attention from the teacher. For us, Christian Meditation allows that attention from the teacher. In teaching Christian Meditation we are also teaching students attention, because we have a view that prayer is mostly about the relationship with us and God and with God and ourselves; and the notion of presence. Being present to the Presence is really I think a very powerful way of understanding what stillness and silence is about. You don't have to *think* anything; presence is within us. In the front of our office, we have a little plaque and the plaque says: «Beaten or not beaten God is present». To me it's an ever present reminder that no matter how we understand or we accept or we know that God is within us, God is there. God is the ground of our being and the relationship between God and each of us is such that by sheer grace separation is not possible. God does not know how to be absent. The fact that many people experience the sense of absence or distance from God is the great illusion we are courting. It is the human condition. Our students and teachers, perhaps you, me certainly, experience this separation and distance. It is real, but through stillness and silence this perceived separation does not have the last word. The illusion of separation is generated by the mind and is sustained by the constant noise, the cacophony that goes on in our heads that is created by so many ways that we are constantly busy. Certainly technology is one of those ways that we are always engaged with the world. I want to share an article with you that talks about this marvellous research that's being done in the brain institutes around the world showing what's happening to people's brains physiologically in terms of the impact of a distracted world, particularly access to the internet and technologies having not just a positive impact as we know they can have, but it's also having some significant impacts on the other side, on the shadow side. This article is called «Bombarded with Impulses We're Turning Scatterbrained». The constant distractions and interruptions are turning our students into scatterbrains, meaning they can't concentrate, they can't go deeply, they lose a sense of what they're supposed to be focusing on very quickly. I think teachers today really have to be absolute geniuses in terms of the little time chunks that you put information into so that students can actually engage with that in any sense that it's going to embed within their brains. These are the sorts of things that I think are a warning sign for us today, not just in terms of how we address information technology but in terms of the notion of educating the whole child. If you want to educate for life in abundance, then we must give students that deep knowledge so that they can withdraw and escape the dreadful cacophony that creates dissonance in their life. The aim is for them to find sanctuary, that still quiet place within. Through Christian Meditation sort of experience that allows them to escape if you like that dreadful cacophony that can really I think just create dissonance in their life and you can find sanctuary you can find that still quiet place within and Christian Meditation really does that very well. Through Christian Meditation we allow our students to experience stillness and silence to develop that understanding that it is more important to be than to have.

Our focus in Townsville is that we have adopted and we really want to embed Christian Meditation as a practice not an ad-hoc approach to all the spiritual practices. So it's not just about having our students learn about it, it's really having them to develop the discipline and the practice because that's where the transformational potential lies. That's why we spend a lot of time on Christian Meditation. People ask me, other directors ask me, why don't you do Ignatian spirituality, why aren't you doing Franciscan spirituality, you've got wonderful Franciscan parishes. Our students do get the opportunity to experience that, too, but this is our great commitment at this time to a practice that we think will make a big difference in our student's lives.

Chapter 5

Meditation in Renewing Spiritual Life

DR. CATHY DAY

Why did it happen in Townsville? What happened that made this experience possible? It's probably because at this moment we are working in radically changed cultural circumstances. Australia has been called the most secular country in the world, and I'm not sure that is a compliment. It basically is about a flight from organised religion, but it's interesting that on the other hand, Australians are still hungering for spirituality. Gary D Bouma, Professor of religion and sociology at Monash University, says that Australians are seeking spirituality, are seeking to re-enchant a world that they are disenchanted with, a world that is full of greed.

Basically he reflected on the growth of Christian meditation as one of the big movements, if you like, in renewing spiritual life in Australia. Most recently the statistics suggest that only 9% of young people between the ages of 18 and 25 actually attend any form of religious service during a year in Australia. I think you know there is that sense that time for religion to change is *now*. We should lose heart that people are losing this sense of the spiritual depth that they are crying for. So I think in our schools, where we have in some cases more than

50% non-Catholic, it's really a great gift that many of our students, no matter what their religious background, no matter what their family circumstances, go home and teach their parents to meditate. So there is this new flourishing, there's a renaissance happening I feel because of Christian Meditation.

It is such a powerful thing at this particular point in time. We put $120,000 a year into formation programmes for our teachers and we think that's an excellent investment, and that's just the formation for Christian Meditation. We take them away to some fairly nice locations and every time they are oversubscribed. These are great opportunities for teachers to experience meditation themselves, because ideally we would like teachers to become meditators. We do not insist that you have to meditate yourself to be able to teach meditation. Some people have alternative views on that, that you can only teach meditation if you meditate yourself. A lot of our teachers have become meditators and actually enjoy that experience. But in some circumstances, and particularly with young children, the teacher prefers to have his or her eyes open because it makes the students feel safe. If there is a teacher aid in the classroom it is much easier for the teacher to sit and meditate with the children.

One of the really interesting things that we have done that I think is bearing great fruit is our senior students retreat. We have the opportunity to take a group of senior students from every single one of our Catholic High schools to a retreat up in the rain forest to talk to them and to allow them to experience Christian meditation with a view to then going back to their schools and establishing their own groups. I think at that age, 16 and 17, a lot of students are really wanting that autonomy; they want to be able to do things without a teacher telling them what to do and showing them what to do. Again it is bearing great fruit. There's a boys' college where the local bishop visited only a couple of weeks ago. They've got a meditation group and they invited him to come and meditate with them.

One of the reasons that I think that that's a very powerful thing to do is that when our students leave school and they go off into other training or work there's nothing that actually connects them to anything that will feed and nurture their spiritual life.

A lot of them will not enter into a worshipping community for whatever reasons. Often in universities, certainly in Australia, we're finding that chaplaincy groups are very marginalised and universities are not encouraging anything to do with God. So for students to actually have the gift of meditation that they can do anywhere, anytime, to have the knowledge that they can actually gather a small group around them and establish their own Christian meditation group, that's a powerful gift that they can continue to nurture their spiritual life and perhaps to pass that gift on to other young people as well.

Chapter 6

How Silently the Wondrous Gift is Given

RT REVD JOHN STROYAN

Jesus welcomes children and encourages us to become as children saying «for the Kingdom of Heaven belongs to such as these» (Matt 19:14). I was reading Karl Rahner on theology of children a couple of days ago and he, referring to these words of Jesus, writes Jesus is not glorifying children but identifying with them. Why? Because like Jesus, he writes, «they expect everything from God».

The great poets recognise something of this. Wordsworth in the famous words

> *Trailing clouds of glory do we come*
> *From God who is our home:*
> *Heaven lies about us in our infancy!*
> *Shades of the prison-house begin to close*
> *Upon the growing boy*

Reflecting on this theme of the dangers of adulthood losing the deep inner truth that we are primarily children of God, William Blake in his *Songs of Innocence and Experience* contrasts the freedom, the playfulness, the spontaneity of the child with what can be an oppressive and joy-smothering con-

trol as perceived in the visible Church. He writes in
«The Garden of Love»

> *I went to the Garden of Love,*
> *And saw what I never had seen;*
> *A Chapel was built in the midst,*
> *Where I used to play on the green.*
> *And the gates of this Chapel were shut*
> *And «Thou shalt not», writ over the door;*
> *So I turned to the Garden of Love*
> *That so many sweet flowers bore.*
> *And I saw it was filled with graves,*
> *And tombstones where flowers should be;*
> *And priests in black gowns were walking their rounds,*
> *And binding with briars my joys and desires*

How easy it is in adulthood to lose that Christ-
childness that we are invited into, and indeed in
the Church to be not careful to become an obsta-
cle to the glorious liberty of the children of God
smothering the playfulness, the spontaneity, the
holy boldness, to quote Thérèse of Lisieux, that we
are all invited into.

But none of this is to romanticise or sentimentalise children. All of us who know children or who remember our own childhood know, too, with William Golding, that children are capable of egotism, manipulation, ganging up, and indeed profound cruelty. Yet we recognise, too, that they have something that we might have lost or lost touch with in ourselves. Jesus says: «I thank thee Father thou has hidden these things from the wise and the prudent and revealed them unto babes» (Matt 11:25). There's a Greek proverb: If you want to know the truth ask a child or a fool.

For spiritual health we need children as much as they need us. So I do get a bit worried when I hear, as I quite often do, wonderful devout Christians describing children as «the future of the Church». As if to say, they will be the ones to grow up into proper adult Christians and so ensure the future of the Church. Whilst this may be true at one level it is surely missing the point. «In as much as we welcome a child in Jesus' name, we welcome Jesus himself» (Matt 18:5). Jesus meets us in children as children.

The work of the Holy Spirit is surely to help us to recover and to enter into our primary identity which is not as priest or religious or teacher or even mother or father or son or daughter or brother or sister, but as a child of God. As Paul writes: «God has sent the Spirit of his Son into our hearts whereby we cry "Abba" Father» (Gal 4:6). The spirit helping us to re-discover our primary identity as children of God.

You remember the description John Wesley wrote in his journal after his heart had been profoundly warmed, strangely warmed, in his words, and his life and his ministry was changed so wonderfully and dramatically. He described the experience thus: «I exchanged the faith of a servant for the faith of a child».

In Isaiah's vision of the new creation of paradise restored, of predator and prey at peace with one another when «the wolf will live with the lamb, the leopard will lie down with the goat, the calf and the lion and the yearling together», he writes «and a little child shall lead them» (Isa 11:6ff).

Children, in their openness to contemplation, to Christian Meditation, can and will and, I'm sure, are already becoming a catalyst for our own openness to God and spiritual growth. In the prayer, the stillness, we give space to God, we give space to our own true selves, and indeed we make more space for the other, the one who is different. In the silence of meditation, the barrier Greek and Jew, male and female, adult and child, the divisions of culture and indeed of faith are lowered.

I'll finish with some words from a carol:

How silently, how silently,
The wondrous gift is given!
So God imparts to human hearts
The blessings of his heaven.

Chapter 7

The Way of Simplicity

LAURENCE FREEMAN OSB

Why we can say meditation is part of the universal wisdom of humanity and why it can be practised by anyone at any stage of life is the simplicity of it. Let's just take a moment to reflect upon that simplicity. The word simplicity is related to the Latin word *simplex* which was used also by tailors and cloth merchants to describe how bales of cloths were folded. So if something was folded once it was *duplex,* and the more frequently you folded it of course the more *complex* it became, the longer it took to unfold it till you get back to the completely opened-minded childlike state of simplicity, *simplex* state.

That is the work of meditation. It is unfolding and allowing the mind and the heart to come into a non-self-reflective state, into that state of pure prayer where we are the reflections and the images of God, the light of God. Therefore, the way into this work, the way into this state, must itself be simple. You cannot become simple by increasing our complexity. And that's the simple wisdom of this tradition Ernie and Cathy spoke about, the John Main tradition. John Main might not like that so much but certainly it's a tradition that is associated with him. He certainly saw himself as who he was, as a communicator passing on a tradition that takes us back to the very roots of our Christian faith.

And the teaching of Jesus on prayer would have to be compatible with this practice if we could call it Christian Meditation. The teaching of Jesus —go into the inner room, let go of many words to trust that God knows our needs before we ask, to lay aside our worries and anxieties, to be mindful, to set our mind on God's Kingdom, and to be in the present moment, not to worry about tomorrow— these elements point precisely to this same state of contemplation that enables us to say that Jesus is a teacher of contemplation. He doesn't speak about rules, rituals or regulations. This is what he speaks about when he speaks of prayer. So our meditation is simply the work we do to receive this gift, this innate gift, and children show us just how innate it is, this gift of simplicity, the simplicity of God. God is infinitely simple according to Thomas Aquinas.

So the way into this simplicity is simple. Following the practical wisdom of the early teachers of prayer, we take a single word or a short phrase. We repeat this word or phrase gently, faithfully and attentively throughout the time of the meditation. As the mind wanders or the mind goes in search of answers or solutions or entertainment or daydream or anxiety or stress, all the different occupations of the mind and our emotions will be used to and looking for, as the mind wanders we simply return to the word. We deal with distractions by the saying of the word, by the faithful gentle repetition of the word. Although that might seem to us in our more complex state to be challenging, difficult, impossible, the child approaches it almost I think as play. The child certainly finds it a discipline, but it is a playful discipline. And if we can be a little less uptight about it, a little less success-oriented and a little more playful with it, we will probably find that we get into it as well as they do; certainly better than we might do otherwise.

Choosing the word that we say is important, because we want to stay with the same word all the way through the meditation, and indeed from day to day, in the morning and the evening meditation as well. This allows the word to become rooted in your heart. The great mystical teachers of the *hesy-chast* tradition in the Eastern Church tell us the word becomes rooted in the heart and awakens the state of continuous prayer. The basic theology that we are putting into practice in meditation is that Christ is *in* us, that we *do not know* how to pray, but the Spirit prays within us. So we take the attention off our ideas about our own prayer and we place our attention fully into this silent presence of *Christ's prayer*, the Spirit's prayer, within us.

As Christians we can take the name Jesus, the ancient Christian mantra; or the word Abba, the word that Jesus made sacred in his prayer; or the word we recommend, the word *maranatha*. This is the word that's given to all children. This is how we teach it; it is the same word that we give to somebody on their death bed or five-year-old. This is a very beautiful, not the only, but it is a very beautiful Christian prayer word or mantra.

If you choose that word, say it as four syllables *ma-ra-na-tha*. Articulate the word clearly in your mind and heart. Listen to it as you say it. Give it your full attention. I wouldn't visualise it, but listen to it as a sound and allow the word to lead you from thought to silence. The word means «Come Lord» but we are not thinking about the word as we say it. We are not thinking of Jesus or thinking of God. We are doing something more, which is *being with*. So the saying of the word is an act of our faith. As Christian tradition tells us: The beginning is faith, the end is love. So if you choose this word say it as four syllables, *ma-ra-na-tha*. You could integrate it with your breathing, if that's comfortable, either by saying the word on your in-breath and breathing out in silence, or you can say the first two syllables *ma-ra-* as you breathe in and *na-tha* as you breathe out. The important thing is not to worry about the technique but to be simple about the actual practice as well. So basically, say the word as you find it most comfortable; say it continuously, faithfully. This is important because this is the discipline of it, the leaving of self-consciousness behind. Then be open to the gift that God desires to give us.

Your posture is important. Take a moment to sit with your back straight, feet on the ground. Put your hands on your lap or on your knees so that your physical posture is a kind of sacrament of the whole experience of your mind and of your heart in this time of prayer, so there is a sense of harmony in body, mind and spirit. Close your eyes lightly, relax the muscles of your face, relax your shoulders, sit upright and alert, breathe normally, then silently in your heart begin to say your word.

The word again I would suggest is *maranatha*, *ma-ra-na-tha*.

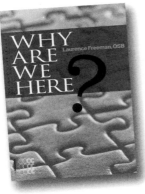

Why are We Here?
LAURENCE FREEMAN OSB
ISBN: 978-1-934996-31-7
80 Pages
Series Meditatio

In this work Freeman examines the radical question of our being in the world. He examines the teachings of John Cassian to show that meditation, with the aid of the ancient Christian tradition of the continuous saying of a mantra, is a path and a discipline to reach this state of simplicity and poverty of spirit of pure prayer called for by the Lord. Freeman also examines the contemplative awakening that is taking place throughout the church fostered in great part by the works of Merton and, especially, Fr. John Main.

Laurence Freeman OSB is a Benedictine monk and Director of The World Community for Christian Meditation. He studied theology at the Universite de Montreal and at McGill University. He was a student of John Main with whom he helped establish the first Christian Meditation Centre in London, dedicated to the practice and teaching of Christian meditation. Freeman is the author of many books and articles including *Christian Meditation; The Selfless Self; First Sight;* and *Jesus: The Teacher Within.*

BUY IT AT: *www.conviviumpress.com*

Meditation with Children

This book was printed on *thin opaque smooth white Bible paper*, using the *Minion* and *Type Embellishments One* font families.

This edition was printed in D'VINNI, S.A., in Bogotá, Colombia, during the last weeks of the second month of year two thousand and thirteen.

Ad publicam lucem datus mense februari in praesentatio Iesu in templo